Applesoft Program Editor

by Richard Hackl

Produced by:
Brian Wiser & Bill Martens

 Apple PugetSound Program Library Exchange

Applesoft Program Editor

Copyright © 1984, 2021 by Apple Pugetsound Program Library Exchange (A.P.P.L.E.)
All Rights Reserved.

www.callapple.org

ISBN: 978-1-6671-6942-2

ACKNOWLEDGEMENTS

Applesoft Program Editor was programmed by Richard Hackl in 1984, with documentation by D. Michael Christensen and Charles Stillman, Ph.D., and originally published by A.P.P.L.E. in 1984.

The Cover and Book were designed by Brian Wiser.

PRODUCTION

Brian Wiser → Cover, Design, Layout, Editing
Bill Martens → Scanning, Editing, Disk Updates

DISCLAIMER

No part of this book may be reproduced, distributed or transmitted in any form or by any means, including photocopying, recording, or other electronic or mechanical methods, without prior written permission of the publisher, except in the case of brief quotations contained in articles and reviews, and program listings which may be entered, stored and executed in a computer system, but not reproduced for publication.

Applesoft Program Editor disk images are available from the publisher: www.callapple.org. No warranty of disk images is made or implied and should be used at your own risk.

Applesoft Program Editor is an independent publication and has not been authorized, sponsored, or otherwise approved by any institution, public or private. All images are under copyright and the property of Apple Pugetsound Program Library Exchange, or as otherwise indicated. Use is prohibited without prior permission.

Apple and all Apple hardware and software brand names are trademarks of Apple Inc., registered in the United States and other countries. All other brand names and trademarks are the property of their respective owners.

While all possible steps have been taken to ensure that the information included within is accurate, the publisher, producers, and authors shall have no liability or responsibility for any errors or omissions, or for loss or damages resulting from the use of the information and programs contained herein.

About Richard Hackl

Richard Hackl was an early 1980s Apple Pugetsound Program Library Exchange (A.P.P.L.E.) member and is the author of *Applesoft Program Editor*, that was first published in 1984 by A.P.P.L.E.. He also was an officer on the A.P.P.L.E. board.

About the Producers

Brian Wiser

Brian Wiser is a producer of books, films, games, and events, as well as a long-time consultant, enthusiast and historian of Apple, the Apple II and Macintosh. Steve Wozniak and Steve Jobs, as well as *Creative Computing*, *Nibble*, *InCider*, and *A+* magazines were early influences.

Brian designed, edited, and co-produced dozens of books including: *Nibble Viewpoints: Business Insights From The Computing Revolution*, *Cyber Jack: The Adventures of Robert Clardy and Synergistic Software*, *Synergistic Software: The Early Games*, *The Colossal Computer Cartoon Book: Enhanced Edition*, *All About Applesoft: Enhanced Edition*, *Graphically Speaking: Enhanced Edition*, *What's Where in the Apple: Enhanced Edition*, and *The WOZPAK: Special Edition* – an important Apple II historical book with Steve Wozniak's restored original, technical handwritten notes. Brian is also the author of *The Etch-a-Sketch and Other Fun Programs*.

He passionately preserves and archives all facets of Apple's history, and noteworthy companies such as Beagle Bros and Applied Engineering, featured on AppleArchives.com. His writing, interviews and books are featured on the technology news site CallApple.org and in *Call-A.P.P.L.E.* magazine that he co-produces as an A.P.P.L.E. board member. Brian also co-produced the retro iOS game *Structris*.

In 2005, Brian was cast as an extra in Joss Whedon's movie *Serenity*, leading him to being a producer and director for the documentary film *Done The Impossible: The Fans' Tale of Firefly & Serenity*. He brought some of the *Firefly* cast aboard his Browncoat Cruise and recruited several of the *Firefly* cast to appear in a film for charity. Throughout these experiences, he develops close personal relationships with many actors, authors, and computer industry luminaries. Brian speaks about his adventures to large audiences at conventions around the country.

Bill Martens

Bill Martens is a systems engineer specializing in office infrastructures and has been programming since 1976. The DEC PDP 11/40 with ASR-33 Teletypes and CRT's were his first computing platforms with his first forays in the Apple world coming with the Apple II computer.

Influences in Bill's computing life came from *Byte* magazine, *Creative Computing* magazine, and *Call-A.P.P.L.E.* magazine as well as his mentors Samuel Perkins, Don Williams, Joff Morgan, and Mike Christensen.

Bill is the author of *ApPilot/W1, Beyond Quest, The Anatomy of an EAMON*, and multiple EAMon adventure games, as well as a co-producer of many books including *What's Where in the Apple: Enhanced Edition, The WOZPAK: Special Edition, Nibble Viewpoints: Business Insights From The Computing Revolution*, and co-programmer for the iOS version of the retro game *Structris*. He has written many articles which have appeared in user group newsletters and magazines such as *Call-A.P.P.L.E.*.

Bill worked for Apple Pugetsound Program Library Exchange (A.P.P.L.E.) under Val Golding and Dick Hubert as a data manager and programmer in the 1980s, and is the current president of the A.P.P.L.E. user group established in 1978. He reorganized A.P.P.L.E. and restarted *Call-A.P.P.L.E.* magazine in 2002. He is the production editor for the A.P.P.L.E. website CallApple.org, writes science fiction novels in his spare time, and is a retired semi-pro football player.

Contents

1. Welcome to A.P.E.

What A.P.E. Does 1
Who Should Use A.P.E. 1
What You Must Already Know 1
Equipment Needed 1
About This Manual 2

2. Learning

How To Begin 3
    How to Copy Diskettes 3
    How to Boot A.P.E. 4
    ProDOS Startup Program 6

Simple Editing 7
    Cursor Moves 7
    Inserting 8
    Deleting 9
    Find 12
    Look 12

Editing Applesoft Programs 15
    Global Editing 15
    Restore 18

Global Search	19
Global Replace	21
Renumber	23
Append	27
Vacuum Packing	29

Advanced Techniques 31

ESCape Cursor Moves	31
Copying	32
Upper and Lower Case	33
Current File Name	34
Embedded Control Characters	35

QuickType 37

About QuickType	37
Using QuickType	38
The QuickType Table	38
A.P.E. for ProDOS vs. DOS 3.3	39
QuickType File Commands	39
QuickType Programming Aids	41
Displaying QuickType Commands	43
Printing QuickType Commands	43
Creating QuickType Commands	43
Deleting Quicktype Commands	46
More Efficient Use of QuickType	48
Keyboard Input in a QuickType Command	49
Saving Changes to the QuickType Table	50
Invisible QuickType Commands	51

3. Reference

Positioning the Cursor 53
    Moving Left Right Up and Down 53
    Jump to Beginning and End of Line 53
    Moving Cursor to a Certain Character 54
    Moving Cursor to a Certain Pattern 54
    Moving Anywhere on the Screen 54

Editing Lines 55
    Insert 55
    Delete 55
    Restore 55
    Global Search 56
    Global Replace 56
    Non-Discretionary Replace 57
    Upper and Lower Case 57
    Embedding Control Characters 57
    Editing Input in a Running Program 58

Copying 58

Renumber / Append 59
    Renumber 59
    Append 62
    Error Messages 63

The Current File Name 65

Using the Monitor 66

Using 80-Columns 67
Using Printers 68
Disconnecting A.P.E. 69
Control Characters 70
Memory Configurations 71
Boot Disk Customizing 72

4. Appendices

    A. Description of Files 73
    B. Memory Map 75
    C. Zero Page Use 77
    D. Quick Reference Card 79

```
             *
          *

       A.P.P.L.E. CO-OP
          PRESENTS
    APPLESOFT PROGRAM EDITOR

    CURRENT CARD IS:
    09) VIEWMASTER ALTERNATE


     *** TO RECONFIGURE ***
       PRESS 'C' IMMEDIATELY

      ******      ******


APPLESOFT PROGRAM EDITOR / PRO
VERSION 2.00 - COPYRIGHT (C) 1988
BY: RICHARD HACKL
```

WELCOME

What A.P.E. Does

Applesoft Program Editor is a popular Applesoft BASIC editor for DOS 3.3 and ProDOS that helps you enter lines and correct mistakes. It works in Applesoft, in the Monitor, and can even be used within the programs you write.

Who Should Use A.P.E.

People who don't use their Apples much may not need A.P.E.. Anyone who spends significant time writing programs on the Apple will likely find A.P.E. quite useful. Programmers have long appreciated the increased productivity that comes with editors. Most programmers doing extensive work in Applesoft or in the Monitor will find A.P.E. to be of tremendous value.

What You Must Already Know

At minimum, you should know how to CATALOG a disk, RUN, LOAD and LIST programs. Understanding a little BASIC will be required in the later portions of this manual. If you don't think you have these skills down pat, a few hours with the introductory manuals that came with your machine should bring you up to speed.

Equipment Needed

A.P.E. runs on the Apple II Plus, IIe, IIc, and IIGS, and III. One floppy disk drive is necessary and a Language Card should also be installed in the Apple II Plus and if you are using an Apple III,

Titan's III plus II Card should be installed. The minimum memory requirements is officially 64K of memory although A.P.E. will run on a 48K Apple II plus. All base commands in A.P.E. will work without the Language Card except RENUMBER and APPEND.

About This Manual

This manual contains these sections:

- Welcome
- Learning
- Reference Guide
- Appendices

If you are using *Applesoft Program Editor (A.P.E.)* for the first time, we recommend that you go through the "Welcome" and "Learning" sections. Once you are familiar with *A.P.E.*, you can use the "Reference Guide" to answer your questions about specific commands and characteristics of this utility. At some point, you may also want to glance at the "Appendices."

Information of special interest has been isolated in separate passages within this manual. Such passages are:

Beginners — Help for those new to computers or Apples.
By The Way — Point of interest not necessary for understanding.
Warning — Information about an area of potential problem.
Review — Review newly-introduced functions.
ProDOS — Features unique to *A.P.E. Pro* for ProDOS.

Passages relating only to one or more of the several Apple machines will be marked appropriately:

```
Apple II
Apple II Plus
Apple IIe
Apple IIc
Apple III Emulation
Apple III plus II
```

2
LEARNING

How to Begin

Disk images can be downloaded from the publisher's site: www.callapple.org/books. Before you do anything, consider making backup copies of all of the diskettes and store the originals in a safe place. As with any new program, you should use a working copy of the A.P.E. master disk, leaving the A.P.E. master disk untouched.

Beginners – How to Copy Diskettes

If you are using a *ProDOS 2.4* or *ProDOS 2.5* master disk, you can also use it to boot from as *Copy II Plus* is included and can be used to perform the A.P.E. disk backup.

Alternatively, insert a *Copy II Plus* boot disk in Drive 1. Boot the drive and when the main menu appears, remove the *Copy II Plus* disk from Drive 1 and insert the A.P.E. floppy disk. If you are using a two drive system, insert a blank floppy into Drive 2. Otherwise, keep the blank handy.

Choose COPY from the *Copy II Plus* menu, then select DISK. Next, choose the source drive and the destination drive. Normally this will be Slot 6 Drive 1 and Slot 6 Drive 2. However, if you are using a single drive system, they will both be Slot 6 Drive 1 requiring you to perform physical disk swapping when prompted by the computer. The system will then copy the floppy disk. Upon completion, remove the blank floppy disk and label it as *A.P.E. Working Backup*.

Warning – Be careful not to mix up your original and blank floppy on a single floppy system as you risk permanent damage to your master floppy.

How To Boot A.P.E.

Booting the *A.P.E. Working Backup* diskette puts A.P.E. into your computer. To boot A.P.E., place your working copy of A.P.E. in Drive 1. If your computer is not on, turn it on now and A.P.E. will be loaded automatically. To start A.P.E. from Applesoft BASIC, enter **PR#6** and press **RETURN**. (This assumes your diskette controller card is in Slot 6). Shortly, your screen should look like this:

```
           A.P.P.L.E.  CO-OP
              PRESENTS
        APPLESOFT PROGRAM EDITOR

        CURRENT CARD IS:
        00) NO CARD IN SLOT #3

        *** TO RECONFIGURE ***
          PRESS 'C' IMMEDIATELY
```

If your computer is capable of displaying 80 characters per line and the CURRENT CARD is NO CARD IN SLOT #3 you will want to reconfigure A.P.E.. To do so, you must press C immediately when you see the opening message. Otherwise, A.P.E. automatically continues booting with the current configuration. If you press C, the disk will whirr briefly, and you will see a menu of 80-column display types. Simply key in the number that corresponds to your 80-column display named on the menu and press RETURN. Once the reconfiguration is complete, the boot process continues normally.

By The Way – If you plan to use an 80-column display, be sure to read the reference section on your 80-column display before turning it on while A.P.E. is active. There are differences how A.P.E. works with certain displays.

Vision 80 card users – The Vision 80 card is not fully compatible with ProDOS. The firmware on this card was customized for use under DOS 3.3. When it is brought up with a "PR#3", it alters memory locations 41516 and 41517, okay for DOS 3.3, but bad for ProDOS. The ESC CONTROL-V QuickType function exists to get around this problem. It saves the contents of memory locations 41516 and 41517, does a "PR#3", and then restores the original values to memory. Any program which turns on the 80-column display with a "PR#3" or equivalent in mid-program will have to be altered to restore the memory locations when running under ProDOS. Future releases of ProDOS may have different values in those memory locations, so you should always get the existing values before the "PR#3".

As the boot process continues, A.P.E. for DOS 3.3 looks like this. For now, press the 0 key. The significance of moving to the Language Card (if you have an Apple II or II Plus) will be discussed later.

```
              A.P.E. VERSION 2.00
              COPYRIGHT (C) 1988
              BY: RICHARD HACKL

   ------------------------------------------

   PRESS THE NUMBER:

      (0) 48K VERSION (NO MOVE)
      (1) MOVE APE ONLY
      (2) MOVE DOS AND APE
```

With A.P.E. Pro, the ProDOS boot screen finishes with:

```
   APPLESOFT PROGRAM EDITOR / PRO
   VERSION 2.00 - COPYRIGHT (C) 1988
   BY: RICHARD HACKL
```

ProDOS Startup Program

This program serves the same function as the HELLO program under DOS 3.3. Since ProDOS occupies the Language Card area of memory as well as the area previously occupied by DOS 3.3, there is only one configuration of the ProDOS version.

Line 120 checks to see if you have *A.P.E. Pro* configured for an 80-column card and automatically switches you to 80 columns when A.P.E. comes up. If you want *A.P.E. Pro* to come up in 40 columns, simply insert a REM at the beginning of line 120 and save the STARTUP program with that change. You may make other changes to the STARTUP program but BE SURE that you MAKE NO CHANGES to lines 7-10 or the program will not function properly.

Simple Editing

Cursor Moves

You could go that way. On the other hand you could go this way. Or you could go both ways...

        - Scarecrow from '*The Wizard of Oz*'

With Applesoft, you can move back and forth within a line, typing over the letters you want to change. The ← and → keys move the cursor left and right. You may also move up and down within your line with the vertical arrow keys. You will find the vertical arrows useful when you create long lines later on.

> **Apple II, II Plus** — Although your computer does not have up and down arrows, A.P.E. provides for you. To move the cursor down, hold down the CONTROL-key and press J. To move the cursor up, use CONTROL-K.

Applesoft will not let you jump quickly to the beginning of the line, but A.P.E. will.

Example – Jumping to Extremes

Type this line, but don't press the RETURN key yet:

```
PRINT "SHE SELLS SEASHELLS BY THE SEASHORE!"
```

Hold down the CONTROL-key and press B. The cursor jumps to the beginning of the line.

```
]PRINT "SHE SELLS SEASHELLS BY THE SEASHORE."
```

Now hold down the CONTROL-key and press N. The cursor jumps to the end of the line. Practice moving the cursor.

Review

←	moves Cursor Left
→	moves Cursor Right
↑ or CONTROL-J	moves Cursor Up
↓ or CONTROL-K	moves Cursor Down
CONTROL-B	jumps to Beginning of a Line
CONTROL-N	jumps to End of a Line

Beginners – Speeding Up the Cursor

What if you want to move the cursor back 20 spaces? Pressing ← 20 times could be tiresome. Applesoft (with or without A.P.E.) provides some help.

> **Apple II, II Plus** – After pressing an ARROW key, hold down the REPEAT key. When the cursor is about where you want, release both keys.

> **Apple IIe, IIc, III Emulation** – By now you probably already know that holding down any key causes it to repeat. Take advantage of this feature when you use the ARROW keys to move the cursor a long way.

Inserting

A.P.E. also lets you insert characters in the middle of a line. CONTROL-I turns on insert mode.

Example – Inserting

Say that the SHE in our story has a sister named Shelley, and Shelley also sells shells at the seashore. You need to update the line:

```
"SHE SELLS SEASHELLS BY THE SEASHORE."
```
to read
```
"SHE AND SHELLEY SELL SEASHELLS BY THE SEASHORE."
```

Using the ARROW keys, move the cursor between the words SHE and SELLS. Hold down the CONTROL-key and press I. Nothing appears to happen. But then type A. Ah ha! You've inserted a character. The line now appears like:

    ]PRINT "SHE ASELLS SEASHELLS BY THE SEASHORE."

with the cursor over the letter A. Now continue typing a SPACE, N, D, S, H, E, L, L, E, Y, and a SPACE. The line looks like this now:

    ]PRINT "SHE AND SHELLEY SELLS SEASHELLS BY THE SEASHORE."

Inserting stops as soon as you type a character that isn't used for text like the ARROW keys, RETURN, or CONTROL-characters.

> **By The Way: Insert Locking** — Normally insert is turned off when you press a non-text character, but there is also a way to lock it on, letting you use the ARROWS to move, then insert, move, insert, and so on. Insert locking is discussed in the reference section of this manual.

You may have noticed that SHE AND SHELLEY SELLS is not quite right. You need to delete the last S in SELLS, without leaving a vacant space in the line.

Deleting

> *Leave! Begone! Depart!*
> *— Queen of the Croonies*
> from '*In Search of the Zipperumpazoo*'

There are five ways to delete with A.P.E.:

Way to Delete #1:

A.P.E. allows you to delete a single character under the cursor by pressing CONTROL-D.

Example – Deleting A Single Character

Let's change the SHE AND SHELLEY SELLS in the line to read SHE AND SHELLEY SELL:

```
PRINT "SHE AND SHELLEY SELLS SEASHELLS BY THE
SEASHORE."
```

Move the cursor over the last S in SELLS. Hold down CONTROL and press D. The S disappears:

```
]PRINT "SHE AND SHELLEY SELL SEASHELLS BY THE
SEASHORE."
```

Beginners – Deleting Faster

You can delete multiple characters by using repetition.

Apple II, II Plus – Hold down REPEAT key while you delete.

Apple IIe, IIc, III Emulation – Consider using your computer's auto-repeat keys as a way to delete a few characters at once. Hold down both CONTROL and D while you delete or hold down DELETE.

Way to Delete #2:

A.P.E. lets you 'X-out' an entire line by holding down CONTROL and pressing X. The line disappears and the cursor is left at the extreme left.

Way to Delete #3:

CONTROL-Y will 'Yank' from the line all characters under and to the right of the cursor.

Way to Delete #4:

CONTROL-Q will "Quit" editing by first deleting all characters to the right and under the cursor, then acting on the commands in the line to the left of the cursor.

Way to Delete #5:

Characters can be wiped out from the cursor to a certain character by pressing CONTROL-W followed by the character you wish the deleting to stop at. The 'stop' character itself is not deleted.

Example – Deleting Up to a Certain Character

Let's change the word SEASHELLS to read SHELLS. Move the cursor over the first E in SEASHELLS:

    ]PRINT "SHE AND SHELLEY SELL SEASHELLS BY THE SEASHORE."

Hold down CONTROL and press W. Now press H. The line should now appear as:

    ]PRINT "SHE AND SHELLEY SELL SHELLS BY THE SEASHORE."

Warning – Until you get used to editing with A.P.E., pay special attention to what is left over to the right of the cursor in your edit line BEFORE pressing RETURN. Unlike regular Applesoft editing, the characters in the edit line to the right of the cursor remain part of the edit line when you press RETURN. For example, if you type: DELETE MYFILE, then change your mind and use the ˆ key to move the cursor back to the beginning of the line and press RETURN… its bye-bye MYFILE! Practice using CONTROL-X, CONTROL-Q, and CONTROL-Y now!

Review

CONTROL-D	Deletes a character
CONTROL-Q	Deletes right of cursor, enters line
CONTROL-Y	Yanks/Deletes everything under and to right of cursor
CONTROL-X	X's the entire line
CONTROL-W	Wipes up to certain character
CONTROL-I	Inserts characters

Find

Another way to position the cursor is with Find. If you hold down the CONTROL-key and press F, the cursor will move in the line to the next occurrence of the character you type. Note that Find only searches forward.

Example – Finding Characters

Position the cursor on the first character of the line PRINT "SHE SELLS SEASHELLS BY THE SEASHORE."

Hold down the CONTROL-key and press F. Now press S.
The cursor moves to the first S in SHE.
Press S again. The cursor is now on the second S.
Press S a couple more times, watch the cursor.

Look

The Find command finds single characters within a line. Sometimes you may want to position the cursor at the start of a pattern of characters. CONTROL-L followed by a pattern does this. CONTROL-N lets you skip to the next instance of the pattern.

Example – Looking for Patterns

Scan the line below looking for the pattern SE:

```
PRINT "SHE SELLS SEASHELLS BY THE SEASHORE."
```

Again position the cursor on the first character of the line. Hold down the CONTROL-key and press L. Now enter the pattern to search for SE. Press CONTROL-N to signal the end of the pattern. The cursor moves to the first SE in SELLS. Press CONTROL-N again. The cursor is now on the SE in SEASHELLS. CONTROL-N again will move the cursor to SEASHORE. One final CONTROL-N takes the cursor to the end of the line.

Review

CONTROL-F	Finds next instance of character
CONTROL-L	Looks for a pattern in a string
CONTROL-N	Next instance of pattern in Look
CONTROL-D	Deletes a character
CONTROL-Y	Yanks everything right of cursor
CONTROL-Q	Deletes right of cursor, enters line
CONTROL-X	X's the entire line
CONTROL-W	Wipes up to a certain character
CONTROL-I	Inserts characters
←	moves Cursor Left
→	moves Cursor Right
↑ or CONTROL-J	moves Cursor Up
↓ or CONTROL-K	moves Cursor Down
CONTROL-B	jumps to Beginning of a Line
CONTROL-N	jumps to End of a Line

EDITING APPLESOFT PROGRAMS

Global Editing

So far you've dealt with the line below in immediate mode only.

```
]PRINT "SHE SELLS SEASHELLS BY THE SEASHORE."
```

Now you'll see how to edit the line when it is incorporated into an Applesoft program.

Beginners – Immediate vs. Program Mode

When a line isn't part of a program, whatever you instruct it to do is done immediately. In Applesoft, this is called the "immediate mode." If a line is preceded by a number, then it is executed when the program it belongs to is run. This is called "program mode."

Moving the cursor, inserting, deleting, and all other A.P.E. editing commands work the same way in Applesoft program mode as they do in Applesoft immediate mode.

To edit a single line in an Applesoft program, you must press CONTROL-E and enter the number of the line you want to edit. Follow the line number with RETURN.

Example – Editing A Single Line Program

Make the seashell s line into an Applesoft program by entering:

```
NEW
10 PRINT "SHE SELLS SEASHELLS BY THE SEASHORE."
```

Run the program by typing RUN.
List the program with a LIST.

Beginners – Entering Applesoft Programs

You've just used the commands NEW, RUN and LIST in the immediate mode, while the command PRINT was used in the program mode. If this is not clear to you, it may be a good idea for you to pause here and work through a little bit of the *Applesoft Tutorial* or equivalent introductory materials.

The program line you've just entered can be edited. Hold down CONTROL and press E. The word EDIT appears. Now press RETURN. The program line is now displayed with the cursor over the first character in the line Use the editing commands you already know to edit the line. Insert a few characters, and then delete them. When you are done editing the line, press RETURN and the line will be accepted as it appears.

A.P.E. lets you step through all the lines of a program, one at a time, beginning with the first. This is done by entering CONTROL-E and RETURN, and again pressing RETURN for each line you want to see. CONTROL-C allows you to stop editing.

Example – Editing Multiple Lines

Add the lines below to the program from the last example (enter each as shown followed by a RETURN, but don't enter the "]"):

```
]5 HOME
]7 FOR I= 1 TO 10
]20 NEXT
]30 END
```

Type LIST and press RETURN. The listing should appear as:

```
]LIST

5 HOME
7 FOR I = 1 TO 10
```

```
10 PRINT "SHE SELLS SEASHELLS BY THE SEASHORE"
20 NEXT
30 END
```

Hold down CONTROL and press E.
Then press RETURN to edit the first line.

```
]EDIT
]5 HOME
```

Press RETURN again, and the second line is presented for editing.

```
]EDIT
]5 HOME
]7 FOR I = 1 TO 10
```

Continue pressing RETURN until all the lines have been reviewed.

If you are editing program lines and decide to quit, just type CONTROL-C. Try stepping through the lines again, but type CONTROL-C when you reach line 30.

What if you don't want to look at all the lines, only a certain line in the middle? You may edit any single line by typing CONTROL-E, entering the line number, and pressing RETURN.

Example – Editing a Single Line

Hold down the CONTROL-key and press E:

```
]EDIT
```

Enter the line number 10:

```
]EDIT 10
```

Press RETURN:

```
]EDIT 10
]10 PRINT "SHE SELLS SEASHELLS BY THE SEASHORE."
```

Move the cursor over the space between SEASHELLS and BY. Press CONTROL-W, and enter a ". " (period character). Then press RETURN. Type LIST and press RETURN to see the effect:

```
]LIST

5  HOME
7  FOR I = 1 TO 10
10 PRINT "SHE SELLS SEASHELLS."
20 NEXT
30 END
```

Restore

Don't it always seem to go that you don't know what you've got 'til it's gone...

— Joni Mitchell

Sometimes you will probably begin to edit a line, and then realize that the line was better off before you changed it. As long as you are still in edit mode, A.P.E. will restore the line to what it was before you bent it all up. You need only press CONTROL-R for Restore.

Example – Restoring A Line

Suppose you are editing a line that reads:

```
]EDIT 10
]10 PRINT "SHE SELLS SEASHELLS BY THE SEASHORE"
```

Now suppose you accidentally erase it by typing CONTROL-X:

```
]EDIT 10
]
```

Still in 'Edit' trying to recover, you type the line back in:

```
]EDIT 10
]10 PRINT "SOMEBODY SELLS SOMETHING SOMEWHERE."
```

18

You just can't remember who sells what where. But then you remember your way out. You press CONTROL-R and the original line reappears:

```
]EDIT 10
]10 "SHE SELLS SEASHELLS BY THE SEASHORE."
```

That's better. You press RETURN to accept the line. Once you have left edit mode, a line cannot be restored.

Global Search

You've already seen how to search a line for a certain character or a certain pattern of characters:

    CONTROL-F   Finds a character within a line
    CONTROL-L   Looks for a pattern of characters within a line

What if you need to find a word not just within the current line, but within an entire program? Using the LOOK command on each line could take a lot of time and typing. A.P.E. supports a Global Find that lets you replace every instance of a character or pattern of characters within an entire program.

Beginners – Global

In this context, Global means throughout the entire program. Global embraces all lines, not just a single line.

To search, you must enter edit mode with a CONTROL-E, hold down both CONTROL and SHIFT, and press the @ key. Then type the characters you are searching for. You may search for up to 30 characters at a time.

Example – Global Search

Load the program SHE SELLS SEASHELLS from your A.P.E. diskette:

```
]LOAD SHE SELLS SEASHELLS
]LIST

10 HOME: VTAB 5
20 PRINT "SHE SELLS SEASHELLS BY THE
   SEASHORE;": PRINT
30 PRINT "BY THE SEASHORE SEASHELLS SELLS
   SHE.": VTAB 12
40 PRINT "COCKLESHELLS, BLUEBELLS,": PRINT
50 PRINT "SHOES, SAILS AND BEDRAILS,": PRINT
60 PRINT "NEVER BY THE SEA SELLS SHE.": VTAB 20
70 END
```

Here's how to search for every occurrence of the word SEA. Hold down CONTROL and press E:

```
]EDIT
```

Now hold down CONTROL and SHIFT at the same time. Press @. Be sure that the @ sign is in inverse video. Enter the word SEA. Press the RETURN key.

```
]EDIT @SEA
]10 PRINT "SHE SELLS SEASHELLS BY THE SEASHORE."
```

The cursor comes to rest on the first letter of SEASHELLS. Press CONTROL-N to see the Next instance which is SEASHORE. Press RETURN to go to the next line that has a SEA in it. The cursor should now be over the word SEASHORE in line 30. Another CONTROL-N moves it to SEASHELLS Press RETURN, and you are out of edit mode because there are no more instances of SEA to search for.

Warning — You may search for patterns of up to 30 characters in length. An attempt to search for a longer pattern results in a high-pitched warning beep and the search is aborted.

A single line may be searched by specifying the line number before the @. Search can be used within a specific range of lines. Follow the EDIT prompt with the numbers of the first and last lines to be searched.

```
]EDIT 20,40 @SHORE
```

The command above will find any occurrence of SHORE including and between lines 20 and 40. You may define an open-ended search starting with a certain line (say line 20):

```
]EDIT 20,@VTAB
```

This command allow you to edit every line in the program containing VTAB from line 20 to the end of the program.

Global Replace

In much the same way you did a global find, you can also do a global replace. First you designate what you want to search for, and then you indicate what you want to replace it with when you find it.

Example – Global Replace

Again load the program SHE SELLS SEASHELLS:

```
]LOAD SHE SELLS SEASHELLS
]LIST

10 HOME: VTAB 5
20 PRINT "SHE SELLS SEASHELLS BY THE
   SEASHORE";: PRINT
30 PRINT "BY THE SEASHORE SEASHELLS SELLS
   SHE.": VTAB 12
40 PRINT "COCKLESHELLS, BLUEBELLS,": PRINT
50 PRINT "SHOES, SAILS AND BEDRAILS,": PRINT
60 PRINT "NEVER BY THE SEA SELLS SHE.": VTAB 20
70 END
```

Try to replace the word SEASHORE with BEACH. Hold down CONTROL and press E:

```
]EDIT
```

Now hold down CONTROL and SHIFT at the same time.
Press @.
Enter the word SEASHORE.
Do another CONTROL-@.
Enter the word BEACH.
Press the RETURN key.

```
]EDIT @SEASHORE@BEACH
]10 PRINT "SHE SELLS SEASHELLS BY THE SEASHORE."
```

The cursor is over first letter of SEASHORE. Now press Y to accept the replacement, or N to skip the replacement. The cursor moves to the next occurrence of SEASHORE. Again A.P.E. pauses to let you accept or reject the replacement.

Like Search, Replace can be used within a range of lines. Just follow the EDIT prompt with the numbers of the first and last lines to be searched.

```
]EDIT 10,20 @SEASHORE@BEACH
```

To search starting at a certain line (say line 10), use the form below:

```
]EDIT 10,@SEASHORE@BEACH
```

Warnings — Both Search and Replace will act on exactly what you type, and nothing more. Pay close attention to upper and lower case, extra spaces, and other subtle differences between what you are searching for and what is really in your program.

When very long lines containing DATA or REMark statements are changed by Global Replace, spaces contained in the DATA or REMark statements may be lost. See the section on "Vacuum Pack."

Renumber

Renumber works only when A.P.E. is in the Language Card (Option 1 or 2 on bootup). If A.P.E. is not in the Language Card then reboot now. Enter this program:

```
]0 HOME
]1 PRINT "SHE"
]2 PRINT "SEASHELLS"
```

The intent was to print SHE SELLS SEASHELLS, but the SELLS was left out. You could solve the problem by inserting the PRINT "SELLS" between lines 1 and 2. But what line number could you give it? You can't get a line in edgewise. To get more room, you must renumber the program. Typically, it would be renumbered to look like:

```
10 HOME
20 PRINT "SHE"
30 PRINT "SEASHELLS"
```

Then you could add PRINT "SELLS" at line 25.

To renumber the program as it is above, hold down both CONTROL and SHIFT and then press ^. Now you will see a # prompt. This lets you know that A.P.E. is ready to renumber. Press RETURN and renumbering will commence. When the Applesoft prompt comes back, you are done. Before renumbering, the program looked like this:

```
]LIST

10 HOME
20 PRINT "SHE"
25 PRINT "SELLS"
30 PRINT "SEASHELLS"
```

Notice that renumber inserted lines 10 line numbers apart from each other. This is called the "Increment" of the line numbers. The increment doesn't always have to be 10. Let's say we want it to be 100 instead of 10. Again, hold down both CONTROL and SHIFT, and enter a ^. Before pressing RETURN, type the letter I and follow it with 100. LIST the program; it should look like this:

```
#I100
]LIST

10 HOME
110 PRINT "SHE"
210 PRINT "SELLS"
310 PRINT "SEASHELLS"
```

This listing can be made a little tidier by also specifying the first line number using the F parameter when renumbering. This time, keep the increment the same but specify a first line number of 100. First, type CONTROL-^ and then type F100, I100. Then list the program.

```
#F100,I100
]LIST
100 HOME
200 PRINT "SHE"
300 PRINT "SELLS"
400 PRINT "SEASHELLS"
```

What if you don't want to renumber the whole program, but only a certain range of lines within a program? This can be done by specifying the starting line (using the letter S) and the ending line (using the letter E).

Example – Renumbering A Range of Lines

Using the program that is in memory from the last example, let's renumber the lines 200 and 300 to become 200 and 210.

First, Type CONTROL-^ and then type S200, E300, F200. End the renumber command with a RETURN. List the renumbered program.

```
#S200,E300,F200
]LIST
100 HOME
200 PRINT "SHE"
210 PRINT "SELLS"
400 PRINT "SEASHELLS"
```

The F is for First line number, and was used here to indicate that you wanted the first renumbered line to have a value of 200.

Almost any time you want to renumber a specific range of lines in a program, you will need the F parameter to indicate what you want the first line number to become.

Notice that the order of the parameters F, I, S, and E is of no importance. The following commands are the same:

```
#F10,I20,S30,E40
#E40,S30,I20,F10
#F20,S30,E40,F10
#S30,E40,F10,I20
```

When you omit the renumber parameters, A.P.E. assumes that F will be 10, that I will be 10, that S will be the very first line existing in the not-yet-renumbered program, and that E will be the last line existing.

By The Way – First Line Versus Starting Line

The renumber parameters that A.P.E. uses (F, I, S, E) are the most commonly used by other renumber programs for the Apple II. People usually have no trouble with Increment and Ending line number, but they often get First line number and Starting line number confused. One way to think of it is this: Starting and Ending go together – they are used to specify a range in the program before it is renumbered. First is what the first line in the range will become after it is renumbered.

Now save the program SHELLS from the previous example, and type NEW. Renumber has two extensions which work hand in hand to simplify the reuse of subroutines in new programs and to assure that nice round starting line numbers for subroutines can be easily preserved. The latter improves the readability of program listings, and extends the useful life of old listings. The REM Renumber extension handles this problem by the use of a special REM statement in the line before the subroutine. Enter the following program:

```
1 GOSUB 50010:REM SET VARS
2 PRINT "PRESS ANY KEY"
3 GOSUB 55010: REM GET KEYPRESS
50 END
50000 REM #50000 VARIABLE SETUP
50010 A=5:B=0:TOTAL=0
50020 RETURN
55000 REM #55000 GET KEYPRESS
55010 GETA$: PRINT
55020 RETURN
```

Oops! We should have tidied up the screen at the beginning of the program but now there is no room. The best solution is to renumber the program to make room for more commands at the beginning.

Try the regular renumber command: Type CONTROL-^, followed by RETURN. This works, but now the subroutines have low and messy line numbers.

Now we'll try REM Renumber, the solution to the messy line number problem. Type CONTROL-^R followed by RETURN. The R is for REM Renumber. List the renumbered program:

```
#R
]LIST

10 GOSUB 50000: REM SET VARS
20 PRINT "PRESS ANY KEY"
30 GOSUB 55000: REM GET KEYPRESS
40 END
49999 REM #50000 VARIABLE SETUP
50000 A:5:B=0:TOTAL=0
50010 RETURN
54999 REM #55000 GET KEYPRESS
55000 GETA$: PRINT
55010 RETURN
```

REM Renumber picks up the starting line number you want for the subroutine from the REM statements. The REM statement itself is given a line number one less than the actual first line of the subroutine.

The increment parameter may be used in REM renumber, but the other parameters (FSE) are ignored.

The REM Renumber command can be used to reorder your subroutines or even larger sections of your programs. All lines after a REM renumber statement and before the next REM Renumber statement can be moved as a block.

Example - Moving Subroutine with REM Renumber

Edit line 49999 from the previous example to read:

```
49999 REM #60000 VARIABLE SETUP
```

Issue the REM Renumber command again. You get a warning:

```
SEQUENCE CHANGED CONTINUE (Y,N)?
```

Type Y and the subroutine is moved.

Warning — You should save your program before you experiment with moving subroutines. Major changes in the organization of a complicated program can produce unexpected results! REM Renumber protects you against creating two lines with the same number, but whenever a line number sequence is changed, you risk mixing together two parts of your program – use it with care.

Append

APPEND, another extension of RENUMBER, allows you to put together pieces of a program from disk. To use this command, type CONTROL-^ as if for RENUMBER but follow it immediately with APPEND and the name of the file to be APPENDed, followed by RETURN. First your program in memory is renumbered beginning at line 10 with an increment of 10, then the second program is APPENDed from disk and renumbered above the old one. This automatic renumbering is necessary to assure that there are no line number conflicts between the program segments.

Example – APPENDing a File from Disk

The previously saved SHELLS program will be APPENDed to the example still in memory. Type CONTROL-^ and the # prompt will appear. Now enter: APPEND SHELLS. The program in memory is renumbered, then the SHELLS program is loaded, renumbered and joined to your current program. The result looks like this:

```
]LIST

10 GOSUB 90: REM SET VARS
20 PRINT "PRESS ANY KEY"
30 GOSUB 60: REM GET KEYPRESS
40 END 50 REM #55000 GET KEYPRESS
60 GETA$: PRINT
70 RETURN
80 REM #60000 VARIABLE SETUP
90 A=5:8=0:TOTAL=0
100 RETURN
110 HOME
120 PRINT "SHE"
130 PRINT "SELLS"
140 PRINT "SEASHELLS"
```

The old line numbering has been lost temporarily to assure space for the APPENDed program. Now REM Renumber can be instructed to move the Seashells message where you want it. Add a line to read:

```
109REM#50
```

Now issue the REM Renumber command again and the program segments fall into place:

```
]LIST

10 GOSUB 60000: REM SET VARS
20 PRINT "PRESS ANY KEY"
30 GOSUB 55000: REM GET KEYPRESS
40 END
49 REM #50
```

```
       50 HOME
       60 PRINT "SHE"
       70 PRINT "SELLS"
       80 PRINT "SEASHELLS"
    54999 REM 1155000 GET KEYPRESS
    55000 GETA$:PRINT
    55010 RETURN
    59999 REM #60000 VARIABLE SETUP
    60000 A:5:B=0:TOTAL=0
    60010 RETURN
```

Now line 40 can be deleted and a new END added as line 80.

Vacuum Packing

Nature abhors a vacuum...

Applesoft sometimes adds unnecessary spaces between many commands for readability. The LIST command in Applesoft always formats the lines you see the same way. You will not be able to determine whether the spaces shown with LIST are really in the program or have just been added by LIST.

Sometimes you may need more room in a line to insert or edit. You may want to compress these extra spaces out. CONTROL-V removes any unnecessary spaces in a line while you are editing it. Any spaces that are part of your text (between quote marks) will not be disturbed.

Warning — If you need to vacuum pack a line containing a DATA or REM statement, put a quotation mark (") immediately after the DATA or REM. Otherwise spaces will be permanently packed out of your DATA or REM statement. During Global Replace long lines are automatically packed, to make room for the changes.

Advanced Techniques

ESCape Cursor Moves

A.P.E. supports an extended version of the Applesoft ESCape editing keys.

Beginners – ESCape mode

In Applesoft, you can move the cursor around on the screen with the following:

ESC A	Right
ESC B	Left
ESC C	Down
ESC D	Up
ESC I	Up
ESC J	Left
ESC K	Right
ESC M	Down

Notice that I, J, K and M form a diamond pattern:

```
    I                  Up
  J   K             Left   Right
    M                 Down
```

The A, B, C and D keys move the cursor one position. To move the cursor again, you must again press ESCape and the A, B, C or D key. The I, J, K M keys leave you in what is known as ESCape mode. After pressing ESC once, you can move the cursor all over with I, J, K and M without needing to press ESC again. In Applesoft, ESCape mode stays in effect until you type any key other than I, J, K M, or the ARROW keys.

Copying

The principal use for the ESC- I, J, K and M keys is to copy text from the screen into the line you're typing. A typical instance of this is LOADing a program by "stealing" its filename from the catalog.

Example – Copying Text From the Screen

Type CATALOG and press RETURN. You'll see something like:

```
]CATALOG

DISK VOLUME 254
A 009 HELLO
B 016 A.P.E.
B 005 ATBL
B 016 MOVE
B 004 CONFIG.APE
A 006 CONFIG.CREATE
B 005 PRINT.QT
B 005 ATBL.ALTERNATE
A 002 SHE SELLS SEASHELLS
```

Type the word LOAD, but don't press RETURN yet:

```
]LOAD
```

Press ESC (don't hold it down) and then press I. A second cursor appears above and to the left of the current cursor (Applesoft uses only one cursor, but A.P.E. uses two – you'll see why soon!) Now press I again. The second cursor moves up. Keep pressing I until the second cursor is on the same line as the SHE SELLS SEA SHELLS program.

Press K to move the second cursor to the right. Keep pressing K until the second cursor lies over the S in SHE. Now press the → key. The second cursor moves off the S and onto the H in SHE. But something else has also happened. A.P.E. has copied the letter S onto the line where your original cursor is.

]LOAD S

Again press → the cursors move, and an H is placed by the S near the original cursor. Press → again.

]LOAD SHE

Press the → key until the whole file name has been spelled out. Then press RETURN.

]LOAD SHE SELLS SEASHELLS

In ESCape mode, A.P.E.'s second cursor can only be moved with the → or with ESC- I, J, K or M. The ← key moves the original cursor, as do all other keystrokes. This means that you can edit the line of the original cursor without ever leaving ESCape mode.

There are times when you may need to move the original cursor to the right without copying text from under the second cursor while you are in ESCape mode. You may do this by pressing CONTROL-S. Otherwise you could exit ESCape mode with ESC-E and then use the → key.

Upper and Lower Case

A.P.E. handles upper and lower case somewhat differently for each Apple.

Apple IIe, IIc — All upper and lower case characters are already available on the Apple IIe and IIc via the SHIFT keys.

Apple II, II Plus, III Emulation — Your Apple II must have a lower case adapter to use lower case in 40 column mode. To get lower case alphas from APE, enter CONTROL-A. All characters you enter will be lower case. While in lower case mode, you may capitalize the next letter by entering a single CONTROL-A followed by the character you want capitalized. To return to all upper case characters, enter two CONTROL-A's in a row.

If your Apple II is equipped with the one-wire shift key modification, then you may use the shift key as on a regular typewriter after you have entered lower case mode with a CONTROL-A.

Beginners – Lowercase Adapters

Lowercase adapters extend your Apple II or II Plus character set to print lowercase letters and a few special symbols. For information on how to install the one-wire shift key modification, see the May 1982 *Call-A.P.P.L.E.* article by Dan Paymar.

Warning – If you don't have a lower case adapter for your Apple II or II Plus, lower case letters will appear garbled.

Current File Name

A.P.E. has a special place to put a file name you are using frequently. Whenever you press CONTROL-P (Put file name), the file name appears. To get the file name into the special place, enter CONTROL-G and type the file name followed by a RETURN.

Example – Using the Current File Name

Hold down CONTROL and type G
Enter "SHE SELLS SEASHELLS" and press RETURN.
Type "LOAD".
Hold down CONTROL and type P.
Press RETURN.

There is room for 30 characters in the Current File Name's special place in memory. You don't have to keep a filename in the Current File Name's special place, you can keep something else there if you like. It is best used for things that change often. There is another mechanism in A.P.E. to deal with commonly used commands that don't change (like CATALOG, LIST, or RUN).

Embedded Control Characters

Sometimes you may wish to embed control characters in your text. The trouble is that A.P.E. uses most of the control characters for editing. How, for example, could you add a CONTROL-D to your text if A.P.E. always grabs CONTROL-D when you enter it and deletes the next character?

Before you enter a control character that you want to include in your text, input a CONTROL-O for Override. If the next character you type is a control character, it will appear in inverse to let you know it has been added. After you press RETURN, the character will disappear from the screen. The character is still in the line, but is no longer visible (as nonprinting characters should be. If you want to see the control characters again, edit the line with CONTROL-E.

Example – Override Control Character

Applesoft rings the bell whenever you use a CONTROL-G with a PRINT. Type PRINT followed by a space and a quote mark:

```
]PRINT "
```

Hold down CONTROL and press O (not zero, but the letter O) Now hold down CONTROL and press G. The G should appear in inverse to indicate it is not a letter G, but rather is a CONTROL-G. Enter CONTROL-O followed by CONTROL-G several more times. Close the statement with another quotation mark.

```
]PRINT "GGGGGGGGGGGG"
```

You should hear the bell beep once for every CONTROL-G you entered.

QUICKTYPE

About QuickType

A.P.E. can help you save keystrokes by using its QuickType Table. Many commands used in Applesoft and DOS require quite a few keystrokes. Frequently used commands, like CATALOG, can be entered with two keystrokes. All QuickType commands are preceded by the ESCape key.

With A.P.E., you can press ESC-Q and the word CATALOG followed by RETURN will be typed for you. This is AP.E's QuickType feature, and ESC-Q is called a QuickType command. In other line editors, QuickType-like features are sometimes called function keys or ESCape sequences.

There are 98 QuickType commands available. Each command is associated with a certain keystroke. Most keystrokes are valid candidates for being associated with a QuickType command. Below are the keys that can't be used:

```
all lower case characters
CONTROL-@
RETURN
ESC
\ | { } ' z
```

It is strongly recommended that you avoid using ESC-A,B,C,D and ESC-I,J,KM for QuickType keystrokes because these are used for pure cursor moves (actually, the Applesoft pure cursor moves are simulated in A.P.E. by being defined as QuickType functions).

Using QuickType

Example – Using QuickType To Get A Catalog

Here's how to get a CATALOG. Press ESC Then press Q. CATALOG and a RETURN is automatically typed for you.

```
]CATALOG

DISK VOLUME 254

A 009 HELLO
B 016 A.P.E.
B 005 ATBL
B 016 MOVE
B 004 CONFIG.APE
A 006 CONFIG.CREATE
B 005 PRINT.QT
B 005 ATBL.ALTERNATE
A 002 SHE SELLS SEASHELLS
```

The QuickType Table

QuickType commands are kept in a table. A.P.E. comes with a selection of commands we have found useful in programming. To see the commands in the QuickType Table, press CONTROL-Z followed by CONTROL-@. Press RETURN to see succeeding pages of the Table. The first character of each line is the Quick-Type command letter. What follows is the text that is actually executed. As you can see, some of the commands are quite involved. For now, we will describe what some of the more important commands do. You do not need to know how they work in order to use them. The Reference section contains a more complete list of QuickType commands.

Warning – Several QuickType commands use Applesoft variable A, thus destroying any existing value for this variable. Before deleting or changing a QuickType command verify that it is not called by other QuickType commands. Commands that are called by others include: CONTROL-C, CONTROL-P, CONTROL-R, ', :, as well as S and P.

A.P.E. for ProDOS vs. DOS 3.3

Several QuickType functions present in the DOS 3.3 version are not necessary under ProDOS and have been eliminated. Others have been changed or added. The space provided for QuickType functions is 400 bytes larger under the ProDOS version than under DOS 3.3.

Filenames and DOS commands differ between ProDOS and DOS 3.3. If you are unfamiliar with ProDOS, you should work through one of the many references available such as *Basic Programming with ProDOS* by Apple Computer, Inc.

QuickType File Commands

Below are the functions at the time A.P.E. version 1.0 was released. In future releases, look for an Applesoft file named INFO.QT which will provide information about changes to the QuickType table.

ESC-1   CATALOGs Drive 1 and displays the number of sectors free on the disk (Sectors free is accurate only when DOS has not been moved to the Language Card).

ProDOS: Does a CAT (the abbreviated CATALOG) on Drive 1.

ESC-2   CATALOGs Drive 2 and displays the number of sectors free on the disk.

ProDOS: Does a CAT on Drive 2.

ESC CTRL-C   *ProDOS:* Does a CAT on the current Drive.

ESC-Q   *ProDOS:* Does a full CATALOG on the current Drive.

ESC-3   LOADs the file from disk with the current filename. Press RETURN to accept the command or CONTROL-X to cancel the command.

ESC-4   SAVEs your Applesoft program to disk using the current filename. Press RETURN to accept the command or CONTROL-X to cancel the command.

ESC-7   *ProDOS:* Supplies the phrase "RENAME". It waits for you to add the rest.

ESC-8   *ProDOS:* LOCKS the "current filename". Press RETURN to complete the command, or CTRL-X to cancel.

ESC-9   *ProDOS:* UNLOCKs the "current filename". Press RETURN to complete the command, or CTRL-X to cancel.

ESC-0   *ProDOS:* Supplies the phrase "DELETE". Add the filename and press RETURN.

ESC-F   *ProDOS:* A lazy person's way to pick up a new "current filename" following a CAT command. Use the "I" key to move the cursor up to the first character of the filename you want, then press RETURN. The file you selected is now the new "current filename".

ESC-S   Space available on disk. Not in *A.P.E. Pro*, as free space is provided by ProDOS.

ESC CTRL-V *ProDOS:* Works around an incompatibility between Vision 80 cards and ProDOS. Turns on the 80-column display if you have a Vision 80 card. This assures that you do not clobber ProDOS.

ESC-W   Displays in hexadecimal the starting address and length of the last BLOADed binary file. (The addresses are accurate only when DOS has not been moved to the Language Card).

ProDOS: now provided in the ProDOS CATALOG.

QuickType Programming Aids

ESC-* : and ;   Effect a CALL-151 to place you in the Monitor from Applesoft.

ESC-@   HOME's the cursor and clears the screen.

ESC-H   Displays in inverse any hidden control characters in catalogs or program listings. Using this QuickType command a second time turns off the control character display.

ProDOS: A.P.E. Pro does not provide for the display of hidden control characters. ProDOS does not allow control characters to be hidden in file names.

ESC-L   Lists your Applesoft Program.

ESC-T   Returns the display to text Page 1 from graphics mode.

ESC →   Is equivalent to pressing the right arrow 10 times. The command finishes with another ESCape. To move right another 10 spaces, press → again. Otherwise press SPACE.

ESC ←   Is equivalent to pressing the left arrow 10 times. The command finishes with another ESCape. To move left another 10 spaces, press ← again. Otherwise press SPACE.

Apple II, II Plus — Several QuickType functions are supplied to produce characters which are not available directly from your keyboard.

ESC-?   Displays the number of characters of space free in the QuickType table. This command works only when A.P.E. is not in the Language Card.

ESC-= BSAVE's the QuickType table. This command will not work when A.P.E. is in the Language Card. Press RETURN to accept the command, CONTROL-X to cancel.

ESC-CTRL-Q Defeats A.P.E., but leaves it resident in memory. This function is useful in situations where you do not want A.P.E. to act on CONTROL or ESCape functions. To reactivate A.P.E. after it has been disconnected, type: CALL 6 RETURN. This function does not actually disconnect A.P.E. from the input and output streams, but does prevent it from actually doing anything.

ESC-P PEEKs the two byte value from the memory location indicated by Applesoft variable A.

ESC-# Performs a decimal-to-hexadecimal conversion (Range 0-65535) from Applesoft. You are prompted with: "A=". Enter the decimal number that you wish to convert. If you make a mistake, press RETURN and start over. The function also PEEKs the two bytes starting at the memory address of the number you entered – handy for getting the values of Applesoft memory pointers.

ESC-$ Performs a hexadecimal-to-decimal conversion (Range $0-FFFFF) from Applesoft. You will be prompted with: *. Enter the hexadecimal number that you wish to convert. If you make a mistake, press return and start over. The function also PEEKs the two bytes starting at the memory address of the number you entered.

By The Way – You are protected from accidentally PEEKing a value in the I/O range of memory ($C000-$CFFF) when doing hex-dec and dec-hex conversions or using the ESC-P function directly. A reference to that address range causes an ILLEGAL QUANTITY error.

Displaying the QuickType Commands

To display the QuickType Commands, press CONTROL-Z CONTROL-@ and RETURN. The first set of commands appears next to the corresponding keys. Keys designated by inverse video are control characters. The first is CONTROL-A the second CONTROL-B, and so on. It is implicit that they are always preceded by ESCape.

Once you have begun to display, you must continue. Pressing any key allows you to see the next set of codes.

While displaying, you may notice several @ signs in inverse video. These are visible substitutes for CONTROL-M or RETURN.

Printing the QuickType Commands

To print the QuickType Commands to paper, turn on the printer and from Applesoft Immediate mode enable the printer with PR#1 RETURN. Now type BRUN PRINT.QT. CONTROL-characters are represented by lower case characters. The ESC character is represented by:] and a RETURN character is represented by @. A backslash (\ ) character is used to mark the end of each line. Occasionally a QuickType command may contain trailing blanks which can pop up the next time input is called for after the QuickType command is executed.

Creating QuickType Commands

You can add your own commands to the QuickType table. Once your command has been added to the QuickType Table, the revised table can be saved to diskette. A.P.E. and DOS must not be in the Language Card when you do this.

Any of the functions can be modified by you. To modify a function key, you first press CONTROL-Z and then the character you want to change. Immediately after the character, enter the new command. RETURN signals the end of your command. As you saw before,

RETURNs that are supposed to be part of the command can be embedded using CONTROL-@. Check that the command has no unintentional (and invisible) trailing blanks as they can produce unwanted results.

It is quite acceptable to put multiple commands into a QuickType function. If you like, you can also have one QuickType function that calls another QuickType function. Functions can be nested up to 4 levels deep. Use the override command (CONTROL-O) to enter the ESCape character into the lines. The ESCape character will appear as an inverse [.

A QuickType command can call itself, creating an endless loop. This loop can be terminated with CONTROL-RESET.

The Current Filename command key can be used with QuickType commands. This offers flexibility far surpassing uses in file commands alone.

Example – QuickType with Current Filename

Let's create a command that lets us LOAD and LIST whatever program is in the Current Filename variable. The command will begin with ESC-G.

First enter the QuickType table with CONTROL-Z.

Enter G as the second letter for the QuickType command.

Enter LOAD for loading the program.

Enter CONTROL-O CONTROL-P CONTROL-@.

CONTROL-P prints the filename, CONTROL@ gives a RETURN.

LIST, CONTROL-P and CONTROL-@ provide the list of the now loaded program. Press RETURN to accept the new command. It should look like this:

)GLOAD P@LIST P@

Test your command by getting a filename (CONTROL-G) and then keying ESC-G.

By The Way – A.P.E. lets you introduce pauses for user input in the middle of a QuickType command. CONTROL-T followed by the maximum number of characters to get causes a pause. The number of characters can be expressed with ASCII characters greater than '0' (ASCII 48). The letter A for example, would wait for 17 characters (ASCII 65 ('A') - ASCII 48 ('0') = 17).

Beginners – Language Card

The original Apple II could only support 48K of memory. Late in 1979, Apple made a special card with an extra 16K of memory: the Language Card. The Apple II does not address the card's memory in the same fashion it addresses its onboard 48K of memory. Part of the memory (4K) is swapped in and out by accessing softswitches at special memory locations. In order to use the extra memory, programs had to be specially written to access the card.

There are still Apple II computers using Language Cards (often called 16K cards or 16K RAM cards). Many Apple II owners don't have 16K cards, and the Apple III emulation mode has Language Card support with the III plus II board from Titan Technologies.

The IIe and the IIc come with a Language Card equivalent built-in. The IIe and IIc still address their upper 16K of memory the same way as an Apple II with a Language Card does. The extra 16K of memory cannot be used by standard Applesoft. It is common to move DOS into the Language Card to take advantage of its space: Applesoft can then use the space the DOS left behind.

A.P.E. resides in memory. It can be within the lower 48K of the Apple II, or it can be moved with DOS into the upper 16K of memory (the Language Card). Before you begin, you should reboot A.P.E.. When you are asked where to put A.P.E. and DOS, you should select:

```
(0) 48K VERSION (NO MOVE)
```

This signals that you do NOT want to load the Language Card with DOS and A.P.E..

> **Warning** – To successfully SAVE the QuickType Table, DOS and A.P.E. must NOT be loaded into the Language Card.

Deleting QuickType Commands

Removing a QuickType command is done by pressing CONTROL-Z <letter> CONTROL-Q, where <letter> is the letter of the function key you want to delete. Essentially, this puts nothing into the function key, and A.P.E. treats it as such.

The QuickType table that comes with A.P.E. has been filled with as many useful functions as space permits. Thus, before you experiment with creating your own QuickType commands, you may need to delete one or two of the existing ones to make space. A QuickType command (ESCape ?) has been provided to tell you how much space you have left in the QuickType Table. Try it. If you have fewer than 50 characters left, we suggest you delete "ESC-W", the command that gives the starting address and length of the last binary program. This will free up about 120 characters of space.

To delete a QuickType command, prepare to edit it then type CONTROL-Q.

Example – Deleting a QuickType Command

To delete the ESC-W command, type CONTROL-Z followed by W CONTROL-Q. This only deletes the command from the table in memory. As long as you don't save the new table to disk, the CONTROL-W function will still be there the next time you boot A.P.E.

To create a new QuickType command, get into the QuickType programming mode (with a CONTROL-Z) and enter the letter you want to associate with the command. If the command already has a value, it appears. Control characters show up as inverse characters. Next you should enter what you want A.P.E. to type (you may use A.P.E.'s commands to edit the existing line) pressing RETURN signals that you are done. If you want QuickType to print carriage RETURNs, they can be entered with a CONTROL-SHIFT @.

All of the normal A.P.E. editing features are available when you change a QuickType function.

Example – Creating A QuickType Command

Suppose you would like to get "TEXT HOME:LIST" every time you press ESC-W. Here's how to add it to the QuickType Table:

Press CONTROL-Z. The QuickType Table prompt appears as a ")". Enter the letter W to signal that ESC-W is the code we want to modify. Now key in the commands "TEXT HOME:LIST" followed by CONTROL-SHIFT@ and press RETURN.

```
)WTEXT:HOME:LIST@
]
```

Test your new QuickType command by pressing ESC and then W.

Example – Editing A QuickType Command

Suppose you wanted to change ESC-F so that it would give you the current value of HIMEM.

Enter QuickType mode with a CONTROL-Z. Now press the F key. To remove the existing command, type CONTROL-Y (remember Y for Yank?). Now enter:

```
PRINT"HIMEM= ";PEEK(115) + PEEK(116) * 256

)FPRINT"HIMEM = ";PEEK(115) + PEEK(116) * 256@
```

You may insert, delete, jump left, jump right, and so on. As before, you should signal your completion by pressing RETURN or CONTROL-Q.

More Efficient Use of QuickType

QuickType commands can be called from within other QuickType commands. Several general QuickType commands were created for this purpose. For example, ESC CONTROL-P is used for PEEKing two-byte values from memory.

Example – Calling Another QuickType Command

Edit the HIMEM example by entering CONTROL-Z F. Delete the existing command with CONTROL-Y, and enter:

```
A=115:?"HIMEM=";
```

Then type: CONTROL-O ESC CONTROL-O CONTROL-P CONTROL-@. The CONTROL-O's are necessary for entering control characters into the QuickType line. The result should be:

```
]

)FA= 115:?"HIMEM=";[P@
```

Now press ESC-F. The result is:

```
]
A= 115:?"HIMEM=";PEEK(A) + 256 * PEEK(A + 1)
HIMEM=34304
```

Keyboard Input in a QuickType Command

The ability to accept and operate on keyboard input while a QuickType command is executing offers possibilities for some general-purpose QuickType commands. QuickType pauses for input from the keyboard when it encounters a CONTROL-T followed by another character to indicate how many keypresses to accept. The actual number (N) is related to the ASCII value of this character [N=(ASCII value)- 48]. Thus, the characters 1-9 are taken at face value, while the character A causes acceptance of 17 characters, X accepts 42, etc.

Only limited editing is available during QuickType Input. Pressing ← erases the last character entered, but two keypresses (the erased character and the ←) are both counted toward the total specified in the QuickType command. Therefore, when you define QuickType Input commands, you may wish to set a large limit. Pressing RETURN terminates a QuickType Input line – you do not need to use all the space reserved.

Example – QuickType Input Command

Let's make the ESC-F function we used to print the value of HIMEM a little more versatile. Edit the HIMEM example again by entering CONTROL-Z F. At the beginning of the command after A= enter CONTROL-O CONTROL-T followed by 5 for the length limit (65534 is 5 digits, the maximum 2-byte location you could choose to PEEK). Next, delete the remains of 115 and delete "HIMEM=";. The result is:

```
]
)FA=T5:?[P@
```

The T is displayed in inverse to signify that it is a CONTROL character. Now press ESC-F. The result is :

```
]
A=
```

QuickType is waiting for input. Enter 115 for the location of the value of HIMEM. The final result will be:

```
A= 115:?PEEK(A)+256*PEEK(A+1)
34304
```

Saving Changes to QuickType Table

To save the QuickType Table, enter the line:

)BSAVE ATBL, A$9A00, L$300

This saves the QuickType table for automatic loading by A.P.E. the next time it is booted.

As a shortcut, ESC-= has been set up to enter the line above.

Warning — If A.P.E. and DOS have been moved into the Language Card, you will not be able to save the QuickType Table. When A.P.E. is booted, it asks you whether or not you want A.P.E. and DOS in the Language Card. If you plan to make permanent changes to the QuickType Table, select:

(0) 48K VERSION (NO MOVE)

Remember that booting will lose any changes you've made in the QuickType Table.

Invisible QuickType Commands

A special QuickType key (Z) has been defined to let you make part of a QuickType command invisible. When ESC-Z is in effect, characters are not sent to the display. Video output resumes only when a non-null PRINT command is followed by a RETURN. (i.e. PRINT " "@ resumes video, but PRINT@ does not).

Example – Invisible QuickType Commands

Try typing the following:

```
CONTROL-Z G CONTROL-O ESC-Z A=5: B=7:
C=A+B: PRINT "C=";C CONTROL-SHIFT @ RETURN
```

It will look like this on the screen:

```
)G[ZA=5:B=7:C=A+B:PRINT"C=";C@
```

The new Quicktype Key G produces this on the display. It's just what we want to show, no more:

```
C=12
```

> *ProDOS:* Invisible QuickType functions are implemented a little differently under the ProDOS version. A first ESC-Z is used to turn off output to the screen. A second ESC-Z must be used to toggle the video back on. See some of the standard QuickType commands for examples of how this works.

Warning – When using Invisible QuickType in your own QuickType commands, be sure to have an appropriate PRINT command at the end. Otherwise, the video remains off. No harm is done directly. The video can be restored in a variety of ways: pressing CONTROL-RESET causing a ?SYNTAX ERROR message, etc. But while blundering about in the dark you might type and execute a harmful command accidentally!

3

REFERENCE

POSITIONING THE CURSOR

Moving Left, Right, Up and Down

The ← and → keys move the cursor one position within the current line. If you try to move left beyond the end of the line, the cursor will stop at the line's end.

The ↑ and ↓ keys (IIe, IIc, III) move the cursor up and down within the current line.

> **Apple II, II Plus** — The up and down arrow keys can be simulated with CONTROL-J (down) and CONTROL-K (up) keys. While operating in 80-column mode with some cards, these commands will move the cursor 40 characters forward or backward within the edit line.

Jump to Beginning and End of Line

You can jump to the Beginning of the current line by holding down CONTROL and pressing B for Begin.

Jumping to the End of a line is done with CONTROL-N for eNd (recall that CONTROL-E is for Edit).

CONTROL-N is also used to find the next instance of a word with the Look command. After the last instance is found during the look command, CONTROL-N resumes the "END" function.

Moving Cursor to a Certain Character

To find the next instance of a certain character on a line, press CONTROL-F (Find) and follow with the character you want to move to. To Find the next instance, enter the character again. Find is terminated when you enter a different character.

Moving Cursor to a Certain Pattern

To look for a certain pattern within a line, use the Look command. You may enter Look by keying CONTROL-L followed by the pattern you wish to look for.

> **Warning** – Be careful not to press RETURN at the end of the pattern, because A.P.E. will interpret the RETURN to be part of what you are searching for.

Press CONTROL-N to signal A.P.E. that the pattern has been entered. To move to the next instance of the pattern within the line, enter CONTROL-N again.

Look does not search beyond the line itself. The Global Search command is used to search across lines.

Moving Anywhere on the Screen

The standard Applesoft pure cursor moves are supported by A.P.E..

> ESC- A, B, C, and D move a single character position.
> ESC- I, J, K and M enter "ESCape mode" and allow moving several positions.

The moves themselves work nearly the same way as they do in Applesoft without A.P.E., but the ← and → keys work quite differently.

ESCape mode is exited with ESC-E.

The ESCape mode is often used to copy information from the screen into the current input line. For more details, see "Copying."

EDITING LINES

Insert

CONTROL-I allows you to insert characters. It is turned off with a non-text character. If you want to edit without leaving insert mode, use CONTROL-I CONTROL-I. This turns on the insert lock. The ARROW keys can now be used without interrupting insert mode. Insert lock can be turned off with another, single CONTROL-I.

Delete

CONTROL-D   Delete a single character under the cursor.

CONTROL-W <char>   Wipes out all characters up to but not including <char>.

CONTROL-Y   Deletes all characters to the right of the cursor.

CONTROL-Q   Deletes all characters to the right of the cursor quits editing, and acts on the edit line.

CONTROL-X   Deletes all characters in the current line. After CONTROL-X the cursor remains on the same line. CONTROL-X always deletes the input line when editing, but the result is a null output line, producing no effect. If you are editing an existing program line and press CONTROL-X, the program line is left unchanged. To delete a program line, type the line number and press RETURN.

Restore

CONTROL-R   Restores contents of the Applesoft line you are editing to the state it was in before you began. Restore has no meaning in immediate mode.

Global Search

```
CONTROL-E
CONTROL-@ <search pattern>
```

finds instances of patterns within a whole program. The search is always upper/lower case sensitive, so:

```
]EDIT @Print
```

will not find the same phrases as:

```
]EDIT @PRINT
```

Global Replace

A.P.E. can replace a pattern in a program with another pattern.

```
CONTROL-E
CONTROL-@ <search pattern>
CONTROL-@ <replace pattern>
```

CONTROL-@ finds instances of <search pattern> and asks if you want to replace them with the <replace pattern>. Since you have the discretion of accepting or rejecting each instance of the pattern, this is called a discretionary replacement.

If you respond Y for yes, the pattern will be replaced. If you respond N for no, the pattern will not be replaced. Any response other than N will go ahead with the replace.

The form for replacing the command PRINT with XXXX is:

```
]EDIT @PRINT@XXXX@
```

Non-Discretionary Replace

If you want the replace to proceed without responding to each case, add an extra CONTROL-@ to the end of the line.

```
EDIT @PRINT@XXXX@@
```

This replaces all instances of PRINT with XXXX. The changes are displayed on the screen as they occur, but you aren't asked if you want the replacement to occur – it happens whether you want it to or not. In a desperate situation, you could lessen the impact of an unwanted global replace by pressing CONTROL-C repeatedly until the operation was finished. Imagine how much damage you can do to your program with this command if you're careless.

Upper and Lower Case

A.P.E. supports upper and lower case input.

Apple II, II Plus – CONTROL-A switches between upper and lower case. Another single CONTROL-A signals that the next character is to be capitalized, and subsequent alphabetic characters are to be in lower case (if the next character turns out to be other than a letter from A to Z, the CONTROL-A is ignored). Two CONTROL-A's lock the machine in upper case, much like on alpha-lock key.

Apple IIe, Apple IIc, III plus II – Shift keys work normally with the IIe and IIc. Do not attempt to use CONTROL-A with a IIe or IIc.

Embedding Control Characters

CONTROL-O (for Override) signals A.P.E. that the next character it gets from the keyboard should not be taken to be an A.P.E. command, but is instead a control character to be embedded in the line.

Suppose you wanted to enter a CONTROL-D into a line. If you try to type CONTROL-D, A.P.E. assumes that you want to delete a letter. If you enter CONTROL-O first, and then CONTROL-D, A.P.E. will know that the next keystroke you type (CONTROL-D) is NOT to be interpreted as an A.P.E. command (in this case, the Delete command).

Editing Input in a Running Program

A.P.E.'s editing commands are always available when input from the keyboard is called for in a running program. If you wish to edit the existing value of a variable in the program, then use this form:

```
<LINE NUMBER>PRINT CHR$(5)<VARIABLE NAME>
: INPUT <VARIABLE NAME>
```

Specifically, a program fragment might look like this. In this example, the existing value of A$ is brought back for editing by line 30:

```
10 INPUT A$
20 INPUT "OKAY? (Y/N)";B$:IF B$="Y" OR
   B$="y" GOTO 50
30 PRINT CHR$(5)A$: INPUT A$
40 GOTO 20
50 END
```

COPYING

When using the pure cursor moves (ESC- I, J, K, M), you can copy text from the copy cursor to the current input line. The → copies text from left to right.

By The Way – Since → is used for copying, it is not possible to move the input line cursor from left to right with the → key when in ESCape mode. To compensate for this deficiency, CONTROL-S can be used to move the cursor to the right without copying.

Remember that A.P.E.'s ESCape mode is not terminated with non-text characters as it is with Applesoft – you can edit the current input line while copying from the copy cursor *without* ever leaving the ESCape mode. Insert delete and other editing commands remain active. You cannot however, edit text on the screen under the copy cursor. Only the text by the input cursor may be edited. Also remember that in A.P.E., ESCape mode is terminated with an ESC-E.

Renumber / Append

Renumber

A.P.E.'s renumber routines allow you to change the line numbers in some or all of your program. You control the range of lines by specifying a start and end of the range. You can control the size of the interval between each of the newly numbered lines, and the value of the first line to be numbered. There is also a special option called REM Renumber which lets you renumber several portions of the program at once using different combinations of renumber options.

There are 5 renumber parameters:

- I - Increment
- F - First new line number
- S - Start of the range to renumber
- E - End of the range to renumber
- R - REM renumber

Most of the parameters above have an argument and a default value:

Option	Lowest	Highest	Default
I - Increment	1	1023	10
F - First	0	63999	10
S - Start	0	63999	0
E - End	0	63999	63999
R - REM Renumber	NA	NA	NA

The first four parameters may be freely intermixed. REM Renumber only allows the Increment parameter to be used. Other parameters are ignored.

A.P.E. MUST be moved to the Language Card (Options 1 or 2 selected during boot-up) to use Renumber.

To perform a Renumber, type CONTROL-SHIFT ^. A # prompt appears. Next enter the parameters in any order separated by commas. Spaces following the commas are allowable:

```
<Parameter><Value>,<Parameter><Value>,
<Parameter><Value>,<Parameter><Value>,
```

When Renumber is working, "####" characters are printed on the screen to indicate that the program is busy. A very long program can take a significant amount of time to renumber.

Warning — Do not interrupt Renumber while it is working. Pressing RESET could cause the loss of your program from memory.

Example – Using Renumber

To Renumber the program using the defaults (all lines with an increment of 10 and a starting line number of 10), simply press return after getting the # prompt.

To renumber lines 500-1000 with an increment of 50 and move this range of lines to line 9000, after getting the # prompt enter:

I50,S500,E1000,F9000 followed by **RETURN**

The REM Renumber command lets you control the beginning line number(s) of one or several program blocks (usually subroutines) with a single command. When you make changes in one part of the program and run REM Renumber, you do not need to worry about affecting the line numbering in the rest of the program. Use of REM Renumber can greatly extend the life of program listings during program development.

The beginning of each REM Renumber block is marked by a line starting with REM followed by # and the number you want ultimately for the first linenumber of the block. (Spaces are allowed between #and the number; titles or comments may be added after the number).

The end of a block is defined by: (1) the end of the program or (2) a REM# <linenumber> statement marking the beginning of the next block. REM Renumber assigns < linenumber > to the line following the REM statement. The REM statement itself is assigned a line number one less than that. Thus, GOSUBs to the routine can refer to the first line that actually does anything.

Example – Using REM Renumber

```
10 GOSUB 110:GOSUB 130:GOSUB 150:GOTO 160:END
100 REM #3000
110 PRINT "HOT":RETURN
120 REM #2000
130 PRINT "CROSS":RETURN
140 REM #1000
150 PRINT "BUNS":RETURN
160 PRINT "THIS WAS THE END OF THE PROGRAM"
```

When a REM Renumber is performed on this program, you are prompted with the message:

```
SEQUENCE CHANGED CONTINUE (Y,N)?
```

In this case, the appropriate response is Y. We have specified that the subroutine that prints HOT (new line 3000) is to come after the routine that prints CROSS (new line 2000).

The REM Renumbered program looks like this:

```
10 GOSUB 3000: GOSUB 2000: GOSUB 1000:
   GOTO 1010: END
999 REM #1000
1000 PRINT "BUNS": RETURN
1010 PRINT "THIS WAS THE END OF THE PROGRAM"
1999 REM #2000
2000 PRINT "CROSS": RETURN
2999 REM #3000
3000 PRINT "HOT": RETURN
```

Care must be taken when sections of the program are moved around (SEQUENCE CHANGED). In this example, the new sequence causes problems. After line 1010 is executed, the program "falls through" into the subroutine at line 2000), causing CROSS to be printed again, followed by a RETURN WITHOUT GOSUB error.

Append

A file on disk may be APPENDed to the end of the Applesoft program in memory by first keying A.P.E.'s Renumber command:

CONTROL-SHIFT ^· When the # prompt appears, then type: APPEND <filename> RETURN, where <filename > is the name of the file you wish to APPEND from disk.

After the APPEND command is executed, the program in memory is automatically renumbered with a starting line number of 10 and an increment of 10. The second program is appended from disk and renumbered (with greater line numbers) above the original program, also with an increment of 10.

> **Warning** – As a precaution, SAVE your program before APPENDing.

Do not interrupt APPEND. To do so could cause the loss of your program from memory. Be patient. Long programs can take significant time to process.

If the automatic Renumber of the Appended program fails for any reason (See error messages below), the Appended program may be left at the end of the original program but with lower line numbers. A program in this condition cannot be repaired easily and should not be used.

Error Messages in Renumber / Append

BAD SYNTAX

Indicates that your command cannot be interpreted. The S,E,F,I,R and APPEND parameters must be in UPPER CASE, separated by a single comma. The APPEND command does not allow any Renumber parameters. In REM Renumber, the BAD SYNTAX message appears if a REM Renumber statement has no <linenumber> specified after the "#" The BAD SYNTAX command always aborts Renumber with no change to the program.

BAD QUANTITY

A Renumber or REM Renumber that would result in an illegal line number (less than 0 or greater than 63999), or that specifies an illegal increment (less than 0 or greater than 1023) causes the BAD QUANTITY message. Renumber is aborted with no change to the program.

BAD LINE

Renumber has found a reference to a nonexistent line number in one of your statements containing GOTO, GOSUB, ONERR GOTO, ON GOTO, or ON GOSUB when the BAD LINE # error message appears. Renumber continues, but the bad line number reference is set to 0 (e.g. GOTO 0). Make a note of the line number where the error occurred so that you can fix the bad reference.

LINE TOO LONG

Applesoft lines must not be longer than 239 characters. Renumber can cause the linenumber itself to grow, and line number references (GOTOs, GOSUBs, etc.) within the line to get bigger. The total line length can be pushed over the 239 character limit. A.P.E. warns you: "POSSIBLE CRASH. CONTINUE (Y /N)?." A CRASH renders your program unusable. Answer "N" and Renumber is aborted with the program left unchanged. You should split up the offending line into two shorter lines before proceeding with Renumber.

By The Way — When the LINE TOO LONG test is done by Renumber, it assumes all result line numbers will be five digits long. Often this is an overestimate. It may be safe to answer Y to the "POSSIBLE CRASH CONTINUE (Y/N)?" prompt if you know the problem line will not be too long after Renumbering. This is sometimes the case when ON GOTO contains a long linenumber list with many references to low line numbers. In such instances, always SAVE the program before attempting Renumber, and always LIST the entire program after the Renumber is complete to verify it has come through intact.

POSSIBLE CRASH CONTINUE (Y/N)?

See LINE TOO LONG

DUPLICATE LINE NUMBER

If your Renumber command would cause two lines to be given the same number, you will see the DUPLICATE LINE NUMBER message and Renumber is aborted. Look for these problems:

REM Renumber: You may have inserted too many lines in the section of program before a REM # <linenumber> line. Try again specifying a smaller line number Increment or change the <linenumber> value to avoid a conflict. A DUPLICATE LINE NUMBER conflict may also be created when subroutines are moved around by changing the <linenumber> values. Remember to allow room for the effect of Renumber on the previous section, since REM Renumber changes numbering in the entire program.

Standard Renumber: When you specify different values for the Start and First parameters in Renumber, this can result in a line or block of lines being moved in on top of others.

SEQUENCE CHANGED CONTINUE (Y/N)?

When Renumber would create a different ordering of lines in you program, you are given a chance to change your mind. Be sure that the change in ordering doesn't disrupt the way your program will run If your answer is "N", the Renumber is aborted.

OUT OF MEMORY

Renumber requires only a modest amount of memory space to work. If your program to be renumbered is extremely large or the combined size of the program in memory and a program you are Appending is too large, Renumber may have inadequate workspace. When you get the OUT OF MEMORY error message, the Renumber / Append command is aborted.

> **Warning** – Check your program for problems if you get the OUT OF MEMORY message while doing an APPEND. Depending on when memory is exhausted, only the original program may have been renumbered. If the error occurs after the second file is LOADed successfully, this portion of the program may be left with lower line numbers than the first portion. This is an unrecoverable situation without expert knowledge of Applesoft's internal workings. Do not try to use a program left in this condition.

CURRENT FILE NAME

A.P.E. has a special function key that will hold a string of characters. When A.P.E. first comes up, this variable has the A.P.E. version and copyright notice in it, but you can change it to hold whatever you wish. Originally it was meant to hold a filename that is to be used frequently or in QuickType functions.

CONTROL-P accesses the variable and prints it out on the screen.

CONTROL-G signals A.P.E. that the next characters typed are to be loaded into the variable. RETURN signals the end of the characters to be added.

Using the Monitor

The Monitor is a program built into the motherboard of every Apple II. It allows you to view and change the contents of the Apple's memory. There are a few different versions of the Monitor, but all versions are nearly the same.

You can enter the Monitor by typing:

```
]CALL -151
*
```

The asterisk that appears instead of the bracket (]) prompt lets you know that you are in the Monitor. To leave the Monitor you must enter 3D0G and press RETURN.

The *Apple II Reference Manual* includes a brief tutorial on the use of the Monitor.

A.P.E. is still active when you enter the Monitor. Many of the A.P.E. editing commands work as they did in Applesoft. The standard Monitor commands can be used, but you must precede them with a CONTROL-O for Override CONTROL character. The Monitor commands are:

```
CONTROL-O   CONTROL-E           Display 6502's registers
CONTROL-O   CONTROL-Y           Jump to subroutine at $3F8
CONTROL-O   CONTROL-B           Enter Applesoft
CONTROL-O   CONTROL-C           Reenter Applesoft
<slot> CONTROL-O   CONTROL-P    Divert output to device
<slot> CONTROL-O   CONTROL-K    Access Input from device
```

By The Way – Leaving the Monitor. For your convenience, CONTROL-C can be used alone, without having to type the CONTROL-O first.

Using 80-Columns

Before using your 80-column display with A.P.E., you must press "C" for CONFIGURE when A.P.E. first boots, then choose your 80-column display card on the menu. The information is automatically saved to your disk for the next time you boot A.P.E. The PR#3 command turns on your 80-column display as usual from Applesoft. Please see "Exceptions" below regarding the function of your particular display.

A.P.E. supports these boards and environments:

    Videx VideoTerm
    Videx UltraTerm
    IIe 80-Column Card
    IIc 80-Column Mode
    Applied Engineering ViewMaster-80
    Vista Vision-80 Card

Exceptions

A few of the 80-Column cards have limitations when running with A.P.E. When using the Videoterm, Ultraterm, and ViewMaster-80, the ↑ and ↓ keys (CONTROL-K and CONTROL-J) yield backward and forward cursor moves of 40 spaces respectively.

The Vista Vision-80 card should not be used in the DOS Move mode. The card modifies memory in the range of normal DOS 3.3 when it is turned on.

Using Printers

A.P.E. is active even when you have issued a PR#1 and each output line is printed on the printer. Any control codes used for setting margins and the like must be preceded by CONTROL-O when you are operating in immediate mode. For example, if you type CONTROL-I 80N, the CONTROL-I is interpreted as an INSERT command by A.P.E. To send the intended command to the printer, you would type: `CONTROL-O CONTROL-I 80N`.

When A.P.E. is taking keyboard input in immediate mode, contrary to Applesoft alone, it doesn't actually pass on any characters to the printer until you key in the carriage return at the end of the line. The margin width command above is effective but gives you a SYNTAX ERROR message which also prints on the printer. If you terminate the line with CONTROL-X, A.P.E. cancels the entire line before the printer gets any of it. It is better to send printer commands in immediate mode using the form:

`PRINTCHR$(9);"80N"`

This method avoids getting a SYNTAX ERROR message. If you are more adventuresome, you could create a QuickType function to send the command. The following sample QuickType command (ESC-G) avoids all visible output on the printer but sends the desired margin command:

`)G[Z PRINTCHR${9);"80N"@`

The "[Z" stands for CONTROL-O ESC-Z, and "@" stands for CONTROL-SHIFT @.

DISCONNECTING A.P.E.

You may wish to disable A.P.E. when testing or running some programs. The procedure varies depending on whether or not A.P.E. has been moved to the Language Card. Memory location 994 indicates the current configuration.

    PEEK(994) = 96 (A.P.E. not moved)
              = 00 (A.P.E. moved to the Language Card)
              = 01 (A.P.E. and DOS moved)

To disable A.P.E.:

    POKE 39376,255 (A.P.E. not moved)
    POKE 992,255 (A.P.E. moved)

POKE the same location with a value of 0 to re-enable A.P.E..

A QuickType function (CONTROL-Q) has been provided to disconnect A.P.E. in all configurations. See the QuickType Section for details.

Warning — A.P.E. could best be described as dormant when it has been disabled. It ignores commands, but can affect the operation of some programs. Some utilities do not work properly when used with A.P.E., even when it is disabled. *FID* works unreliably when A.P.E. is moved. *COPYA* does not work properly when DOS has been moved to the Language Card.

Control Characters

Control characters hidden in program lines and disk Catalogs can be displayed by using the A.P.E. Control Find feature. When it is enabled, control characters show up on the screen in Inverse video. This may be used in the 40-column display mode only.

A location is POKEd to turn on Control Find. The location depends on whether or not A.P.E. has been moved to the Language Card. See "Disconnecting A.P.E." for how to identify the current configuration.

To enable Control Find:

    POKE 39377,255 (A.P.E. not moved)
    POKE 993,255 (A.P.E. moved)

POKE the same location with a value of 0 to disable Control Find.

MEMORY CONFIGURATIONS

There are three basic configurations of A.P.E. that can be used.

The first configuration leaves DOS and A.P.E. both in main memory. On 48K Apple IIs and on Apple II is without the "III plus II" card, this is the only version that works. A major disadvantage of this 48K configuration is that HIMEM: has been moved downward 4K bytes for A.P.E.. This means that there is 4K less room in memory for Applesoft programs. Another significant disadvantage is that A.P.E.'s renumber is not available.

The second configuration moves A.P.E. from main memory to the Language Card. Renumber is also placed in the Language Card. HIMEM: is left undisturbed.

Like, the second configuration, the third configuration moves A.P.E. from main memory into the Language Card. The difference is that DOS itself is also moved to the Language Card. This configuration then moves HIMEM: up above the space that was occupied by DOS, giving your Applesoft programs much more room than is ordinarily available. The use of this room is transparent to you as an Applesoft programmer; you don't have to do anything special to use it.

When DOS is moved into the Language Card the default MAXFILES is 2. If more buffers are needed and MAXFILES is increased. space is allocated below $BF00 (48896 decimal) and HIMEM is moved down.

> **Warning** — The INIT command is disabled when DOS is moved to the Language Card. Some programs such as *COPYA* and *FID* do not work properly when either A.P.E. or DOS has been moved to the Language Card.

Boot Disk Customizing

You may wish to create a special A.P.E. disk for day-to-day work. Only three files are needed to successfully boot A.P.E.: HELLO, A.P.E., and ATBL.

If you configure A.P.E. to run in the Language Card, you will also need the MOVE program. All files on the A.P.E. disk can be safely transferred to another disk using *FID* or *COPYA*. (Note that these disk utilities do not work reliably when A.P.E. is active running in the Language Card). You may delete the nonessential files. If you need to reCONFIGURE A.P.E. later on, you will be prompted to insert a disk containing CONFIG.APE if the file is not on the boot disk.

If you decide that you will always use a particular A.P.E. memory configuration, a line in the HELLO program can be changed to AUTOSTART, so you don't have to tell HELLO which configuration you want each time. Line 1000 contains a DATA statement with two variables:

```
1000 DATA 1,0
```

If you want A.P.E. to AUTOSTART, then set the first variable to 0, and the second to the value of the memory configuration you want. For example, if you change the line to read:

```
1000 DATA 0,2
```

then A.P.E. and DOS will automatically be moved to the Language Card on boot-up.

Warning — Before making any other changes to the HELLO program, see "Appendix A: Description of A.P.E. Files" for more information.

4

APPENDICES

DESCRIPTION OF FILES

HELLO

The HELLO program brings in other necessary files, installs A.P.E., and offers the user options for changing the video card or memory configuration.

This program is open to change by you, but with some restrictions. Do not add to, delete or change anything before line 11. The CONFIG. APE program transfers information directly to line 9, and it is assumed the line is in a particular memory location.

The end of the HELLO program must not be extended beyond location 7920 ($1EF0), or be longer than 22 disk sectors.

You may wish to have multiple QuickType tables for a variety of programming tasks. A menu could be created in the HELLO program to let you select the appropriate table.

ATBL and PRINT.QT

ATBL is the QuickType Table which is installed in A.P.E. by the HELLO program. This file is handled separately from A.P.E. to make it easy for you to have more than one QuickType table. ATBL is $300 (768 decimal) bytes long, and is located at $9A00 (39424 decimal) when A.P.E. is not moved to the Language Card. Alternate QuickType tables may be BLOADed to this location at any time when A.P.E. is running in the non-moved configuration.

PRINT.QT can be BRUN to print the contents of the QuickType table. Control characters are shown as lower case characters. The ESCape character is represented by:] and a RETURN character is represented by @.

ATBL.ALTERNATE

ATBL.ALTERNATE is a more compact though less readable version of ATBL. All PEEKs and POKEs are done via nested QuickType functions, calling ESC ← and ESC → respectively. This frees up 30 characters for more QuickType functions. Beginners may find this file a little intimidating. If you wish to look at the table, type:

```
BLOAD ATBL.ALTERNATE,A$9A00 RETURN
```

when using the 48K configuration of A.P.E.. If you wish to use this as your regular QuickType table, then the filename should be changed to ATBL (after renaming the existing ATBL file to something else).

A.P.E. and MOVE

A.P.E. is the heart of the editor. MOVE is a temporary file brought in by HELLO to move A.P.E. and DOS to the Language Card. Neither file should be modified.

CONFIG.APE and CONFIG.CREATE

CONFIG.APE modifies A.P.E. to work with various 80-column displays. The program is automatically BRUN by the HELLO program when you press "C" as A.P.E. is booting.

CONFIG.CREATE is an Applesoft program to aid the addition of more 80-column display drivers. When this program is RUN, it updates the drivers in CONFIG.APE.

Memory Map

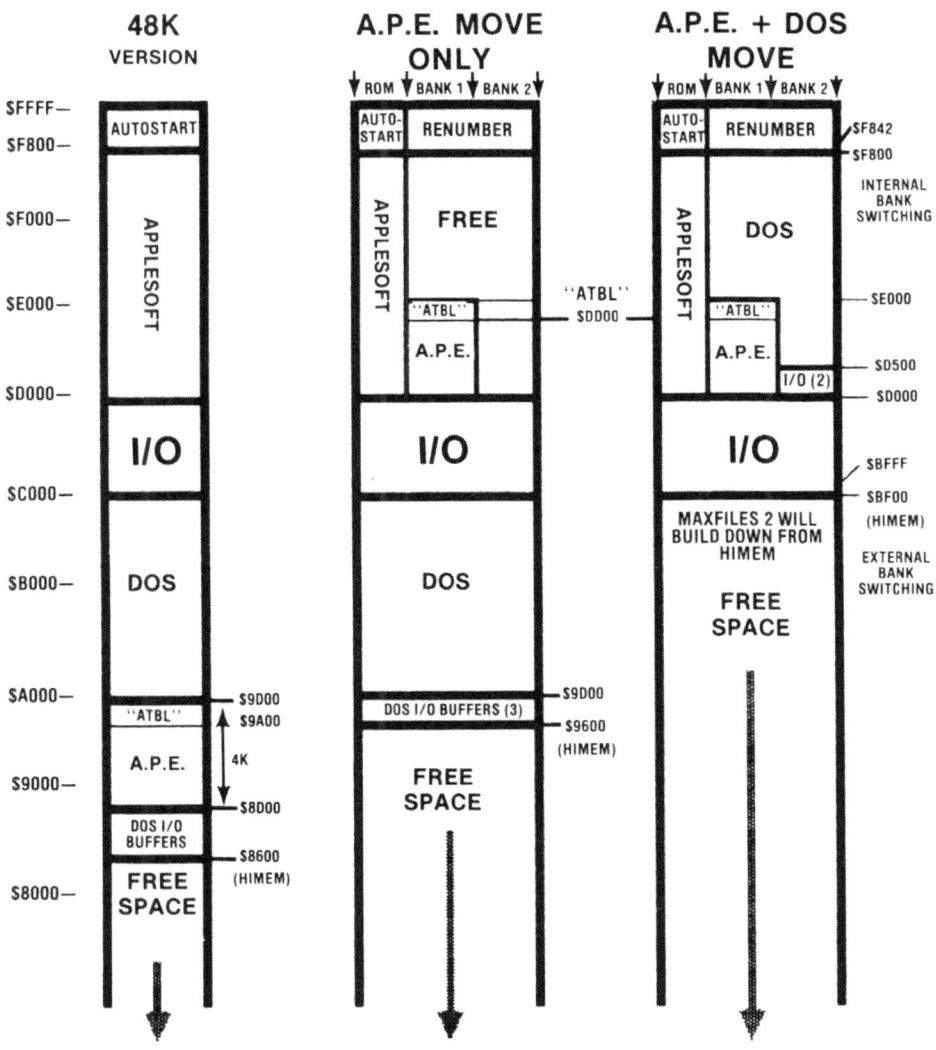

A.P.E. Pro for ProDOS uses the same Zero Page memory locations as the DOS 3.3 version. Since, ProDOS occupies the Language Card area of memory, *A.P.E. Pro* can have only one memory configuration (shown below).

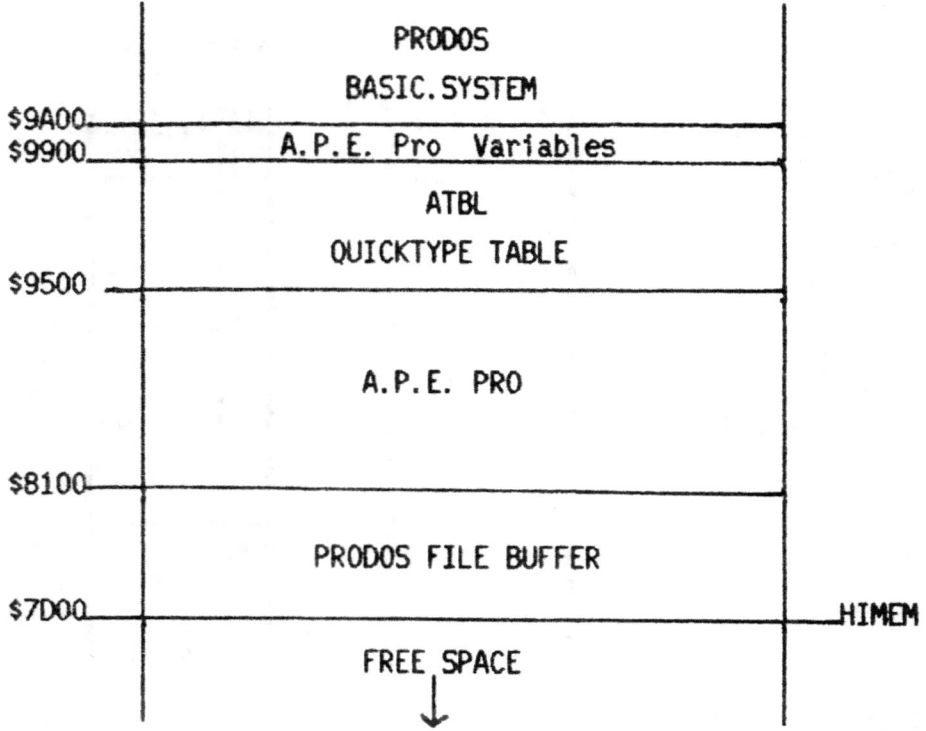

Zero Page Use

Most of A.P.E.s Zero Page use is temporary: Some other locations are used widely by major A.P.E. subroutines and should be approached cautiously. A few locations are used for permanent variables and should not be used at all by your routines. A.P.E. also affects the usual Monitor and Applesoft locations in the course of editing ($21, $23-$25, $28-$29, $50-$51, $9E-$9F, $B1, $B8-$B9).

The following locations are used for temporary variables by A.P.E.. Original values are not restored by A.P.E. These locations should be safe to use for temporary variables in your routines at any time:

Quite safe for your routines:

$19-$1A (Used by Append) $EB-$ED, $FA-$FC

Used heavily by many A.P.E. routines, but possibly okay:

$06-$09 (QuickType Function Editing, Renumber, Global Edit)

Do not use:

$FD-$FF (Permanent variables)
$EE-$EF (Used in QuickType)

Warning — This information is provided for Assembly Language programmers. It is believed to be accurate, but use these locations with caution. Be especially careful when using Zero Page locations in QuickType functions.

If your machine language program uses Monitor routines for getting input A.P.E. will be active and use its Zero Page locations. To be safe, disconnect A.P.E. upon entry to your routine and reconnect A.P.E. upon exit.

Quick Reference Card

Move cursor left	←, CTRL-H
Move cursor down	↓, CTRL-J
Move cursor right	→, CTRL-U
Move cursor up	↑, CTRL-K
Repeats arrow key pressed	Arrow-REPT (II, II Plus)
Repeats arrow key pressed	Arrow [held down] (IIe, IIc, III)
Jump to beginning of line	CTRL-B
Jump to end of line	CTRL-N
Find a character within line	CTRL-F <char to find>
Look for a pattern within line	CTRL-L <find pattern> CTRL-N
Skip to next Look instance	CTRL-N
Delete a single character	CTRL-D
Delete under and to right of cursor	CTRL-Y
Delete right of cursor, accept line	CTRL-Q
Delete up to a character	CTRL-W <char>
Delete entire line	CTRL-X
Delete multiple characters	CTRL-D REPT (II, II Plus)
Delete multiple characters	CTRL-D [held down] (IIe, IIc, III)
Insert mode on	CTRL-I
Insert mode off	any non-text character
Insert lock on	CTRL-I CTRL-I
Insert lock off	CTRL-I
View QuickType Table	CTRL-Z CTRL-@
Edit QuickType Key	CTRL Z <char>
QuickType command RETURN char	CTRL-@
Pause for input on Q.T. command	CTRL-T <# of chars to get>
Get current filename	CTRL-G <filename>
Print current filename	CTRL-P

Override next control char	CTRL O <control char>
Vacuum pack a line	CTRL-V
Upper/lower case toggle	CTRL-A
Upper case lock	CTRL-A CTRL-A
Enter global edit	CTRL-E < optional range>
Leave global edit	CTRL-C
Global search	CTRL-E CTRL-@ <search>@
Discretionary global replace	CTRL-E CTRL-@ <search>@ <replace> @
Accept replace	Y, any key except N or RESET
Reject replace	N
Non-discretionary replace	CTRL-E CTRL@ <search> @ <replace> @ @
Restore previously edited line to old state (UNEDIT or RESTORE)	CTRL-R
Edit every instance word specified by {sequence}	CTRL-E SHIFT @{sequence}
Move cursor right	ESC-A
Move cursor left	ESC-B
Move cursor down	ESC-C
Move cursor up	ESC-D
Enter ESCape mode	ESC
ESCape mode left	J
ESCape mode down	M
ESCape mode right	K
ESCape mode up	I
End ESCape mode	ESC-E
Copy from copy cursor to input	→
Move input cursor right	CTRL-S

RENUMBER   CONTROL-^
Renumber/Append program in memory   CTRL-SHIFT-^

    Increment   I <value>,
    First destination line#   F <value>,
    Starting line to renumber   S <value>,
    Ending line to renumber   E <value>,
    REM Renumber   R,
    Append a file from disk   APPEND <filename>
    Renumber by 10 (Default)   RETURN at # prompt

F,I,S,E can be combined by comma separator

www.ingramcontent.com/pod-product-compliance
Lightning Source LLC
Chambersburg PA
CBHW070810220526
45466CB00002B/617